A Paines Plough and Ro

Half-Empty Glasses

by Dipo Baruwa-Etti

Paines Plough

ROSE
THEATRE

Supported by
**ARTS COUNCIL
ENGLAND**

Half-Empty Glasses

by Dipo Baruwa-Etti

Cast

TOYE Samuel Tracy
REMI Princess Khumalo
ASH Sara Hazemi

Production Team

Director Kaleya Baxe
Designer Ryan Dawson Laight
Composer and Sound Designer Roly Botha
Casting Director Annelie Powell CDG
Lighting Designer Rory Beaton
Lighting Programmer and Lighting Associate Jack Ryan
Movement Yami Löfvenberg
Assistant Director Joelle Ikwa
Company Stage Manager Verity Clayton
Deputy Stage Manager Charlotte Smith-Barker
Production Manager Guy Ongley
Touring Technician Zak Brewin
Touring Technician Jack Scanlon

DIPO BARUWA-ETTI (Writer)

Theatre includes: *The Sun, the Moon, and the Stars* (Theatre Royal Stratford East); *An unfinished man* (The Yard Theatre). Film includes: *The Last Days* (BBC/BFI Network/Tannahill Productions); *The Madness* (The Mono Box). Dipo has been shortlisted for the George Devine Award, Alfred Fagon Award, and as a poet has been published in *The Good Journal*, *Ink Sweat & Tears*, *Amaryllis*, and had his work showcased nationwide as part of End Hunger UK's touring exhibition on food insecurity.

KALEYA BAXE (Director)

Kaleya Baxe is a writer, director and facilitator whose work is driven by her passion for representation, inclusion and collaborative kindness. As well as working on outreach and youth projects with the Young Vic, Kiln, and Arcola Theatre, her work often shines a light on important subjects such as five-star (*Guardian*) show *Patricia Gets Ready (for a date with the man that used to hit her)* and has toured schools, youth settings and pupil referral units (Written/Little Fish Theatre). As an assistant she has worked with acclaimed writers such as Chinonyerem Odimba (Artistic Director, Tiata Fahodzi) and Mike Bartlett (*Doctor Foster*, *Life*). Kaleya was the Paines Plough Trainee Director for 2020/21 and is currently working on her first writing commission exploring 'Black Voices in Myth' with company Actors of Dionysus.

Her work as a director includes: *Queens of Sheba* by Jess Hagan (LAMDA); *Hear Myself Think* by Olly Gly (audio series available on Spotify); *786* by Ric Renton (Paines Plough R&D/LAMDA); *Patricia Gets Ready (for a date with the man that used to hit her)* by Martha Watson Allpress (VAULT Festival Show of the Week Award Winner); *Written* by Alex Cooke (Little Fish Theatre, schools and youth settings tour).

SAMUEL TRACY (Toye)

Samuel Tracy is a recent graduate of the Royal Academy of Dramatic Art. They also trained at The BRIT School receiving qualifications in Theatre and Dance. Samuel is also a Deviser/Theatremaker and won the 'Strawberry Picking' New writing Best Play award for *Branches, Twigs and Synapses*.

Theatre includes: *Romeo and Juliet, Sticky* (Southwark Playhouse); *Dr. Jekyll & Mr Hyde* (Rose Theatre); *Zigger Zagger* (Wilton's Music Hall); *Orfeo* (Royal Opera House/ Roundhouse).

Television includes: *Woke Overnight* (BBC).

SARA HAZEMI (Ash)

Sara Hazemi is a British-Iranian actor and writer from London. She is thrilled to be a part of this year's Roundabout season, and to share these stories with audiences across the UK. Theatre credits include: *Tales from Hans Christian Andersen*, *A Midsummer Night's Dream* (Guildford Shakespeare Company); *The Little Mermaid* (Fever); *Oedipus at Colonus* (Cambridge Arts Theatre); *Othello* (European theatre tour); *A Series of Improvable Events* (The Cambridge Impronauts/Edinburgh Fringe/ Gilded Balloon).

Television credits include: *This Is Going to Hurt* (BBC); *The Cockfields* (Gold).

PRINCESSS KHUMALO (Remi)

Princess Khumalo is a Zimbabwean-born actor who graduated from LIPA in 2021. Princess is very excited to be a part of Paines Plough Roundabout rep season. She has featured in CBBC's *So Awkward*. Since graduating from LIPA, Princess has starred in BBC *Doctors*, and also filmed a lead part in a UKTV comedy pilot, *Holier Than Thou*, which is set to be aired on DAVE this summer. Princess has also been lucky enough to have toured the north with various Liverpool production companies including: All Things Considered Theatre Company, Out The Attic Theatre Company, and Falling Doors Theatre in collaboration with Everyman and Playhouse Theatre.

RYAN DAWSON LAIGHT (Designer)

Theatre includes: *My Son's A Queer (But What Can You Do?)*, *Torch Song* (Turbine Theatre); *My Brilliant Friend* (National Theatre, Associate Costume Design for Soutra Gilmore); *Pinocchio*, *The Wizard of Oz*, *Crossing Lines*, *Sleeping Beauty*, *Beauty and the Beast*, *Peter Pan*, *A Christmas Carol*, *Grimm Tales*, *The Tiger Who Came to Tea* (Chichester Festival Theatre). As Associate Designer at Creation Theatre, recent work includes: *Grimm Tales*, *Alice: A Digital Wonderland*, *Don Quixote*, *The Tempest*, *The Snow Queen*, *Peter Pan*, *Brave New World*, *Swallows and Amazons*, *Dracula*, *A Christmas Carol*, *Alice in Wonderland*, *Hamlet*, *Macbeth*, *As You Like It*, *Henry IV*, *King Lear*, *Treasure Island*. For Le Gateau Chocolat: *Duckie* (Royal Festival Hall); *Icons* (Edinburgh Festival); *Black* (Unity Theatre Liverpool/Soho Theatre); *Le Gateau Chocolat* (Menier

Chocolate Factory); *HMS Pinafore*, *Chess*, *Blondel*, *The Mikado* (Union Theatre national tours); for The BRIT School: *Landmines* (Ovalhouse), *Sticky*, *Infinite Joy* (Southwark Playhouse); *Chip Shop The Musical* (Octagon Theatre Bolton); *Ice Cream Opera* (Freedom Arts Studio).

Dance includes: *Botis Seva's BLKDOG* (Sadler's Wells, Olivier Award Best New Dance 2019); *Blak Whyte Gray* (Boy Blue/Barbican, Olivier Award Nomination 2018); *REDD* (Boy Blue/Barbican Theatre); *Madhead* (NYDC/Sadler's Wells); *Wasteland*, *Coal* (Gary Clark Company, UK Theatre Award for Achievement in Dance); *Toro*, *Mariposa*, *Ham and Passion* (DeNada Dance Theatre); *Drew McOnie's Drunk* (Leicester Curve/Bridewell Theatre); *Good Morning Midnight* (Jermyn Street Theatre); *Genius* (Anjali); *New Ways Of Living* (Pink Fringe Brighton); *Je Suis* (Aakash Odedra Company/ Lillian Baylis Studio, Sadler's Wells); *Ruffle* (Carlos Pons Guerra/Rambert Dance/Lowry Theatre); *Hear Hear* (Deaf Men Dancing/Sadler's Wells).

ROLY BOTHA (Composer and Sound Designer)

Roly is a composer and sound designer and they're proud to be an associate artist of The PappyShow. Theatre includes: *Coming to England* (Birmingham Rep); *Orlando* (Jermyn Street); *WILD* (Unicorn); *Muck* (Park Theatre); *Blowhole* (Soho Theatre); *Milk & Gall* (Theatre503); *Fritz & Matlock* (Pleasance London/ Edinburgh Fringe Festival/Pleasance Edinburgh); *Helen* (BAC); *Brother* (Southwark Playhouse); *Warheads* (Park Theatre; 2020 Olivier nominated); *BOYS, GIRLS, CARE* (The PappyShow/national tour); *Making*

Fatiha (Camden People's Theatre). Audio includes: *It's A Practice Podcast* (The PappyShow); *Plays For Today* (Southwark Playhouse). Trans people, especially black trans femmes, are being discriminated against more than ever. Please consider donating to the charities Gendered Intelligence or Not A Phase.

ANNELIE POWELL CDG (Casting Director)

Theatre credits include: *House of Shades*, Vassa (Almeida); *Coming to England, What's New Pussycat?* (Birmingham Rep); *Wendy and Peter Pan* (Leeds Playhouse) as well as recent work for Hampstead Theatre, Hull Truck Theatres, Hoxton Hall, Theatr Clwyd, Headlong, Royal and Derngate Northampton, English Touring Theatre and the Bush Theatre.

For Nuffield Southampton Theatres as Head of Casting credits include: *The Audience, Billionaire Boy, The Shadow Factory, Don Carlos, Fantastic Mr Fox, A Streetcar Named Desire* (Nuffield Southampton Theatres/Theatr Clwyd/English Touring Theatre). For the Royal Shakespeare Company credits include: *Hamlet, King Lear, Imperium, Myth, The Rover, Seven Acts of Mercy, Two Noble Kinsman, Wendy and Peter Pan, Oppenheimer* (RSC/West End, co-casting).

Annelie's television work includes: projects with Netflix, Apple, Warner Brothers, BBC, ITV and Nickelodeon, alongside her work on independent feature films and adverts.

RORY BEATON (Lighting Designer)

Rory is a freelance lighting designer working both in the UK and internationally. He has previously

been nominated for a Knight of Illumination Award for his work on *Così fan tutte* at Opera Holland Park. He is also a recipient of the Michael Northen Award, presented by the Association of Lighting Designers. Previous projects include: *For Black Boys Who Have Considered Suicide When The Hue Gets Too Heavy* (Royal Court); *I Love You, You're Perfect, Now Change* (London Coliseum/Broadway HD); *Lovely Ugly City* (Almeida); *Spike, Kiss Me Kate* (Watermill); *Dishoom!* (UK tour); *Summer Holiday, The Rise and Fall of Little Voice* (Bolton Octagon); *Edward II* (West End); *Macbeth, La Bohème, Elizabeth I, The Marriage of Figaro, Dido & Aeneas, Amadigi, Il Tabarro, Idomeneo, Radamisto* (English Touring Opera); *West End Producer - Free Willy!* (Cuffe & Taylor); *60 Miles by Road or Rail* (Theatre Royal Northampton); *Tumble Tuck* (King's Head); *The Blonde Bombshells of 1943, Summer Holiday, A Christmas Carol* (Pitlochry); *How Love is Spelt* (Southwark Playhouse); *Skylight, The Mountaintop* (Chipping Norton/tour); *Maklena* (tour); *70 Års Opera* (Danish National Opera); *A Christmas Carol* (Belgrade/Chipping Norton); *Little Women, L'amico Fritz, The Cunning Little Vixen, Così fan Tutte, L'arlesiana, Manon Lescaut, Le Nozze di Figaro* (Opera Holland Park); *Dubliners* (OTC Ireland); *Mad Man Sad Woman* (Head for Heights). Rory has also designed projects with Blenheim Palace and The British Library. www.rorybeaton.co.uk

JACK RYAN (Lighting Programmer and Lighting Associate)

Jack is a freelance Lighting Programmer, Designer and Associate working both in the UK and internationally. His credits as lighting programmer include: *Choir of Man* (West End); *Macbeth, Elizabeth I, Idomeneo, Amadigi, Dido and Aeneas, Jonas, Radamisto* (English Touring Opera); *Christmas @ Blenheim Palace* (Sony/Culture Creative), as well as companies including: Crossroads Entertainment, Selladoor, Immersion Theatrical and Rambert Dance Company. Jack also works in live broadcast and commercials including work for companies such as: Peloton, Samsung, EA Sports and Vanish.

Previous design credits include projects for Smyle with companies such as BMW, Samsung and Abbey Road Studios (artists incl. AlunaGeorge and Gavin DeGraw); *Blood Upon the Rose* (Hammersmith Apollo, SEC Armadillo, The Gaiety Theatre) and regularly designs a range of performances at Union Chapel, Islington. Jack is also the Associate Lighting Designer for the West End production of Choir of Man.

Jack has also worked with artists such as Becky Hill, Celeste, Nao and Laura Mvula.

YAMI LÖFVENBERG (Movement Director)

Yami Löfvenberg is a movement director, theatre director and a multidisciplinary artist working in the intersection of movement, theatre and cross-arts. Between making her own work, Yami mentors educate and deliver workshops nationally and internationally. She is currently the lecturer on the first-ever Hip-Hop module at Trinity Laban Dance Conservatoire. A British Council and Arts Council England recipient, Howard Davies

Emerging Directors Grant Recipient, One Dance UK DAD Trailblazer Fellow, Marion North Recipient, and a Talawa Make Artist. She was on the creative choreographic team for the 2012 Olympics Opening Ceremony and is a member of performance collective Hot Brown Honey.

Movement director credits include: *The Concrete Jungle Book* (Pleasance); *Kabul Goes Pop* (Brixton House); *Human Nurture* (Theatre Centre/Sheffield Theatre); *Athena* (The Yard Theatre); *Notes On Grief* (Manchester International Festival); Rare Earth Mettle, Living Newspaper (Royal Court); *Fuck You Pay Me* (Bunker); *Breakin' Convention* (Sadler's Wells); *Talawa TYPT* (Hackney Showrooms); *Boat* (BAC). Director credits include: *Fierce Flow* (Hippodrome Birmingham); *Kind of Woman* (Camden People's Theatre); *Afroabelhas* (Roundhouse/British Council/Tempo Festival, Brazil). Assistant director/choreographer credits include: *Hive City Legacy* (Roundhouse, Home, Millennium).

JOELLE IKWA (Assistant Director)

Joelle Ikwa is an aspiring Director and is delighted to be working as a Trainee Director with Paines Plough, as part of her three month placement with RTYDS. Joelle is assisting all three plays for the Roundabout 2022 season. Her journey began in Coventry at the Belgrade Theatre over ten years ago, where she went from a youth company member, workshop facilitator, assistant director to director. Joelle wants to share stories that empower and make a difference. With experience as a youth violence intervention worker, Joelle is passionate about raising awareness around issues that affect young people such as knife crime and mental health. Theatre being Joelle's creative conduit, she finds fulfilment in the positive impact that it has on people. Touring through the placement on Roundabout will add to Joelle's knowledge as she's burgeoning in this journey.

Acting credits include: *The Tempest* (Belgrade Theatre); *Coventry Moves* (City of Culture). Assistant Director credits include: *This Little Relic* (BBC); *Nothello* (Belgrade Theatre). Director credits include: *Transcend* (Bramall Music Hall).

VERITY CLAYTON (Company Stage Manager)

Verity has worked in theatres across the UK and abroad – mooring her narrowboat nearby when possible! Theatre includes: *Sorry You're Not a Winner* (Paines Plough/Theatre Royal Plymouth); *The Storm Whale* (York Theatre Royal/The Marlowe); *The Snail and the Whale* (Tall Stories/West End/Sydney Opera House); *Alice and the Little Prince* (Pleasance, Edinburgh/Lyric Hammersmith); *The Journey Home* (Little Angel/Beijing); *There's a Rang Tan in my Bedroom*, *The Singing Mermaid*, *WOW! Said the Owl* (Little Angel); *Under the Rainbow* (Polka Theatre/Galway and Wilderness festivals); *Recycled Rubbish* (Theatre Rites).

CHARLOTTE SMITH-BARKER (Assistant Stage Manager)

Charlotte studied English Literature and Film at Aberystwyth University and Malmo University in Sweden. Upon graduating in 2018, she completed the association of British Theatre Technicians Bronze Award. When not working in theatre, Charlotte teaches English as a foreign language. Theatre includes: *The Catherine Tate Show* (West End); *Clybourne Park* (Park Theatre); *Soho Cinders* (Charing Cross Theatre); *The Sweet Science of Bruising* (Wiltons Music Hall).

Paines Plough

Paines Plough is a touring theatre company dedicated entirely to developing and producing exceptional new writing. The work we create connects with artists and communities across the UK.

'The lifeblood of the UK's theatre ecosystem.' *Guardian*

Since 1974 Paines Plough has worked with over 300 outstanding British playwrights including James Graham, Sarah Kane, Dennis Kelly, Mike Bartlett, Sam Steiner, Elinor Cook, Vinay Patel, Zia Ahmed and Kae Tempest.

Our plays are nationally identified and locally heard. We tour to over 40 places a year and are committed to bringing work to communities who might not otherwise have the opportunity to experience much new writing or theatre. We reach over 30,000 people annually from Cornwall to the Orkney Islands, in village halls and in our own pop-up theatre Roundabout; a state of the art, in the round auditorium which travels the length and breadth of the country.

'That noble company Paines Plough, de facto national theatre of new writing.' *Daily Telegraph*

Furthering our reach beyond theatre walls our audio app COME TO WHERE I'M FROM hosts 180 original mini plays about home and our digital projects connect with audiences via WhatsApp, phone, email and even by post.

Wherever you are, you can experience a Paines Plough Production.

'I think some theatre just saved my life.' @kate_clement on Twitter

 **PAINES PLOUGH** **ROUNDABOUT**

'**A beautifully designed masterpiece in engineering.**' *The Stage*

ROUNDABOUT is Paines Plough's beautiful portable in-the-round theatre. It's a completely self-contained 168-seat auditorium that flat packs into a single lorry and pops up anywhere from theatres to school halls, sports centres, warehouses, car parks and fields.

We built ROUNDABOUT to tour to places that don't have theatres. ROUNDABOUT travels the length and breadth of the UK bringing the nation's best playwrights and a thrilling theatrical experience to audiences everywhere.

ROUNDABOUT was designed by Lucy Osborne and Emma Chapman at Studio Three Sixty in collaboration with Charcoalblue and Howard Eaton.

WINNER of Theatre Building of the Year at The Stage Awards 2014

'**ROUNDABOUT venue wins most beautiful interior venue by far @edfringe.**' @ChaoticKirsty on Twitter

'**ROUNDABOUT is a beautiful, magical space. Hidden tech make it Turkish-bath-tranquil but with circus-tent-cheek. Aces.**' @evenicol on Twitter

ROUNDABOUT was made possible thanks to the belief and generous support of the following Trusts and individuals and all who named a seat in Roundabout. We thank them all.

TRUSTS AND FOUNDATIONS
Andrew Lloyd Webber Foundation
Paul Hamlyn Foundation
Garfield Weston Foundation
J Paul Getty Jnr Charitable Trust
John Ellerman Foundation

CORPORATE
Universal Consolidated Group
Howard Eaton Lighting Ltd
Charcoalblue
Avolites Ltd
Factory Settings
Total Solutions

Paines Plough

Joint Artistic Directors and CEOs   Charlotte Bennett & Katie Posner
Associate Artistic Director   Jesse Jones
Interim Executive Producer   Ellie Claughton
Incoming Executive Director   Jodie Gilliam
Producer   Lauren Hamilton
Outgoing Producer   Tanya Agarwal
Incoming Producer   Ellie Fitz-Gerald
Digital Producer   Nick Virk
Marketing and Audience Development Manager   Manwah Siu
Assistant Producer   Ellen Larson
Assistant Producer   Gabi Spiro
Administrator   Katie Austin
The Big Room Playwright Fellow   Mufaro Makubika
Press Representative   Bread & Butter PR

Paines Plough Limited is a company limited by guarantee and a registered charity.
Registered Company no: 1165130
Registered Charity no: 267523

Paines Plough, 38 Mayton Street, London, N7 6QR

office@painesplough.com
www.painesplough.com

 Follow @PainesPlough on Twitter

 Like Paines Plough at facebook.com/PainesPloughHQ

 Follow @painesplough on Instagram

 Donate to Paines Plough at justgiving.com/PainesPlough

Rose Theatre is the largest producing theatre in South West London and has established itself since its 2008 opening as one of the most exciting theatres in the UK.

Recent Rose Original productions include: *Leopards* by Alys Metcalf, directed by Christopher Haydon and co-produced with Fleabag producer Francesca Moody Productions; *The Seven Pomegranate Seeds* by Colin Teevan, directed by Melly Still; Jeff James and James Yeatman's acclaimed adaptation of Jane Austen's *Persuasion* featuring an explosive foam party and a soundtrack of Frank Ocean, Dua Lipa and Cardi B; the critically acclaimed *Captain Corelli's Mandolin*, adapted by Rona Munro, which transferred to the West End in July 2019 following a successful UK tour; and the world premiere stage adaptation of Elena Ferrante's Neapolitan Novels, *My Brilliant Friend*, adapted by April De Angelis, which transferred to the National Theatre in November 2019. Both were directed by Rose Associate Artist Melly Still.

Forthcoming Rose Original productions include: Bertolt Brecht's masterpiece *The Caucasian Chalk Circle*, in a new version by Steve Waters with songs by Michael Henry and direction by Christopher Haydon, being developed in association with MGC; a brand-new retelling of Charles Dickens' timeless classic, *A Christmas Carol*, adapted by Morgan Lloyd Malcolm, featuring a female Scrooge and a wealth of local talent from the Rose Youth Theatre.

The Rose is home to one of the largest youth theatres in the country, offering over 1,200 participants training, careers advice and the opportunity to take part in productions alongside professionals.

Kingston Theatre Trust, Company Limited by Guarantee. Registered in England and Wales.
Company Registration No. 02497984
Registered Charity 1000182

Rose Theatre, 24-26 High Street, Kingston, KT1 1HL
+ 44 (0) 20 8174 0090

info@rosetheatre.org
rosetheatre.org

Follow @RoseTheatre on Twitter
Follow @rosetheatrekingston on Instagram
Like Rose Theatre at facebook.com/RoseTheatreKingston
Donate to Rose Theatre at rosetheatre.org/support-us/donate

Half-Empty Glasses

Dipo Baruwa-Etti is a playwright, poet and filmmaker. In 2020, he was shortlisted for the George Devine Award and was the Channel 4 playwright on attachment at the Almeida Theatre. Plays include *The Sun, the Moon, and the Stars* (Theatre Royal Stratford East), which was shortlisted for the Alfred Fagon Award for Best New Play, and *An unfinished man* (The Yard Theatre, London). For screen, he wrote and directed the award-winning short film *The Last Days* (BFI Network/BBC/ Tannahill Productions) and has several original projects in development. As a poet, he has been published in *The Good Journal*, *Ink Sweat & Tears* and *Amaryllis*, and had his work showcased nationwide as part of End Hunger UK's touring exhibition on food insecurity.

by the same author

THE SUN, THE MOON, AND THE STARS
AN UNFINISHED MAN

DIPO BARUWA-ETTI

Half-Empty Glasses

faber

First published in 2022
by Faber and Faber Limited
74–77 Great Russell Street
London WC1B 3DA

Typeset by Brighton Gray
Printed and bound in the UK by CPI Group (Ltd), Croydon CR0 4YY

A CIP record for this book
is available from the British Library

978-0-571-38050-3

2 4 6 8 10 9 7 5 3 1

Acknowledgements

Thank you to God, Mum, the siblings, all my family, and those who've been a part of this play's journey – including: Kaleya Baxe, Samuel Tracy, Princess Khumalo, Sara Hazemi, Charlotte Bennett, Katie Posner, Yami Löfvenberg, Joelle Ikwa, Ryan Dawson Laight, Rory Beaton, Roly Botha, Verity Clayton, Charlotte Smith-Barker, Deirdre O'Halloran, Sami Ibrahim, Laura Lindow, Lauren Hamilton, Ellen Larson, Ellie Claughton, Mani Siu, Nick Virk, Jesse Jones, Anne McMeehan, Jim Roberts, Rose Cobbe, Florence Hyde, Dinah Wood, Lily Levinson, Faber, Valentine Olukoga, Cash Holland, Yasmeen Scott, all at Paines Plough and the entire *Half-Empty Glasses* team.

Half-Empty Glasses was first performed at Roundabout in Kingston, in a Paines Plough and Rose Theatre production, on 12 July 2022, with the following cast:

Toye Samuel Tracy
Remi Princess Khumalo
Ash Sara Hazemi

Director Kaleya Baxe
Designer Ryan Dawson Laight
Composer and Sound Designer Roly Botha
Casting Director Annelie Powell CDG
Lighting Designer Rory Beaton
Lighting Programmer and Lighting Associate Jack Ryan
Movement Yami Löfvenberg
Assistant Director Joelle Ikwa
Company Stage Manager Verity Clayton
Deputy Stage Manager Charlotte Smith-Barker
Production Manager Guy Ongley
Touring Technician Zak Brewin
Touring Technician Jack Scanlon

Characters

Toye
sixteen

Ash
sixteen

Remi
sixteen

Adesola
fifty-five

Toye and Remi are Black

Ash is Middle Eastern

Setting

Present day

Various locations

East London

HALF-EMPTY GLASSES

Note

The actors playing Ash and Remi also double as Adesola.

*

Dialogue in bold is spoken to the audience.

A dash at the end of a word or line indicates speech interrupted by the following line.

A dash on its own line indicates a pause. The number of these in a row suggests the duration of the pause, but these can be altered, as directors feel appropriate.

Character names underneath each other without a space indicate two or more characters speaking simultaneously.

Prologue

The stage is bare, with only a piano in the centre. It should largely remain that way.

Toye sits at the piano, in his school uniform, and plays Mozart's Sonata in C. He appears peaceful, happy.

ONE

School gates.
   Toye stands with Ash and Remi, all in their school uniform.

Ash Toye ain't comin to the park.

Remi What? Why?
Toye I've gotta practise.

Ash You're always practisin.
Remi Again?

Toye Got my audition soon.

Remi Still, you can –
Ash You think you're gonna get in?

Toye My tutor thinks so.

   Ash and Remi look at each other and playfully interrogate him.

Ash And you actually wanna go?

Toye I –
Ash It's bare posh, ain't it? Ain't that school bare posh?

Toye Yeah, but –

Ash So why'd you wanna go there?

Toye Their music department's sick and –

Remi So you're just gonna abandon us?

Toye I ain't movin houses.

Ash You'll have new friends though.

Toye Guys, I don't have time for this, I've gotta –

Remi You ain't given us an answer.

Toye Y'know the answer.

Ash Do you, Rem?

Remi Nah, do you, Ash?

Ash Nah.

Remi What's the answer, Toye?
Ash What's the answer, Toye?

Toye You're both so jarrin, y'know?

Remi (*laughs*) Why you avoidin the –

Toye I ain't gonna abandon you.

Ash Good.

Remi You better not.

Toye I might not even get in.

Ash You get into everything.

Remi Ain't that a word.
Toye No I don't.

Remi Toye.

Toye What?
Remi Don't cap.

Toye I don't, I –

Ash Basketball.

Remi Athletics.

Ash Debate.

Toye (*shrugs somewhat smugly*) **What can I say?
I do get into a lot of things**

but this is different
I need a scholarship if I wanna get into this school
There's bare competition
So I need to practise my piano every moment I get
Or I bet there's no way I'm gettin in

Remi Football too.

Toye Those are four things.

Remi Own it, Toye.
You're the GOAT.

Ash Don't gas him up too much, Rem.
Or his feet won't touch the ground no more.

Toye Fine, five minutes.

Remi Five minutes?

Ash Ten.

Toye Seven.

Remi Twenty.

Toye Thirteen.

Ash Seventeen.

Toye Fifteen.
Remi Fifteen.

They smile at each other.

Toye This happens every day.
But, I'm still killin the piano
and homework
and revision either way
so maybe this is just how it's meant to go.
Work-life balance, right?
Plus, ain't nothin better than spending time
with Remi and Asha hoopin
against the backdrop of a blue sky.

TWO

Toye's sitting room.
 Toye arrives home and is taken aback by Adesola's presence. As they speak, Adesola's voice remains quiet.

Toye Hi, Dad.

Adesola Hello, Toye.
 How was school?

Toye Pardon?

Adesola (*slightly louder*) How was school?

Toye Oh.
 Fine.

 –

You're home early.

Adesola Mmm.

 –

Toye How was work?

 –

He pauses and the silence is mad awkward.
 I dunno what to do.
 He looks upset and I . . .
 He looks like he's bout to cry and I . . .
 I've never seen him cry
 so maybe he's not and that's just . . .
 I dunno.
 I don't recognise him any more.
 I was a kid when he was diagnosed,
 so no one ever spoke to me about it.
 But still even now, they don't,
 even though he can't move like he used to.
 Can't use his voice like he used to.

Adesola Fine. I just came home –

Toye (*moving closer*) Pardon? Sorry, I –

Adesola It's fine, Toye, just leave me.

Toye I'm sorry, I just –

Adesola It's fine.
And don't be sorry.
I'm sorry for shouting, I just . . .
Today was my last day at work.

Toye Your last day?

Adesola nods.

Oh.

–

Adesola Do you want to watch TV?

Toye I've got homework.

Adesola You've got all evening.

Toye Need to do piano too.

Adesola You've got time.

Toye Fine.
Five minutes.

Adesola Thirty.

Toye Thirty?

–

Fine.

Toye sits with Adesola.

This doesn't happen every day
and we both know we've gotta make good memories.
It's bad enough that he was on top

and now's reverting
to being a boy
right in front of my eyes –
something no one deserves.

It's mad,
havin a brain disorder.
Is this what gettin older brings?
More losses than wins.
More trash for bins.
More frowns than grins.

Parkinson's slammed the door down
like an opp
and started shootin
killin everythin Dad loved.
Most recently, work.

He's too young for this.
I always remember him and Mum sayin that.
But that they wouldn't let it
turn everything upside down.
They should earn crowns for managing to get through it.
With love, peace, unease.
Walking through the terrain that should never have been
ours.

In the end, hours – not minutes – went by,
Mum later joining the ride.
Our entire evening erased.
But it didn't matter, being by his side.

THREE

Toye's bedroom.
  Toye and Remi revise with flashcards.

Remi How'd MLK come to national prominence?

Toye He was part of the bus boycott
  after Rosa Parks' arrest.

Remi Where?

Toye Montgomery.

Remi Yep.
  What year was he awarded the Nobel Peace Prize?

Toye Sixty-four.

Remi Yep.
  When and where did he deliver his 'I have a dream'
speech?

Toye March on Washington for Jobs and Freedom,
  twenty-eighth of August 1963.

Remi Tell me a bit about his leadership.

Toye That's not on a card.

Remi But it's what you'll have to do.

Toye Then be more specific.

Remi Toye, tell me –

Toye Just stick to the flashcards I wrote.

Remi Just gimme something.
  Anything.

Toye I, er . . . He was considered a reluctant leader.
  Didn't seek it out.

Remi He also cheated on Coretta apparently.

Toye That ain't on the card.

Remi Bares.

Toye Remi.

Remi Plagiarised too.

Toye Remi.

Remi I'm just sayin.

Toye Well, you're here to help me revise.

Remi Fine.
Toye And why'd you know all this anyway?

Remi My dad told me, innit.
Didn't want me thinkin MLK was some angel,
so I didn't feel like I needed to be
perfect, y'know?

Toye What ordinary person compares themselves to
Martin Luther King?

Remi I ain't ordinary.

Toye Whatever.

Remi We should all get that tea anyway.

Toye Or we could just not learn about MLK all the time.

Remi Yeah, I'd go with that any day.

Toye For real?

Remi Yeah, course.
Toye Thought I was the only one.

Remi Nah, course not.
It gets boring after a while.

Toye As if no one else exists.
We never hear bout other people.

Remi Or just everyday people.

Toye Why would we learn about everyday people?

Remi Cos they're interesting.

Toye I dunno bout that. My neighbour –

Remi Y'know one of my dad's friends
was the first Black UK chef
with a Michelin star?

Toye Dunno what that is.

Remi It's awarded for mad good cooking.

Toye Right.

–

Can we go back to the cards?

Remi Fine.

–

(*Back to flashcards.*) What fellow activist inspired MLK?

Toye Many did, but 'answer' is Gandhi.
They both believed in the peaceful protest.

Adesola enters.

Adesola Toye.
Toye Non-violence, even when –

Adesola Toye.

Toye and Remi turn around, noticing Adesola.

Toye (*moving towards him*) Yes, Dad?

Adesola Have you seen the hammer?

Toye No, why?

Adesola A picture fell and I wanted to put the nail back in.

Toye I can do it later.

–

Adesola Where's the hammer?

Toye I dunno.
  Mum might know.

Adesola I don't wanna ask her.
  She'll start telling me to be careful,
  as if I haven't been doing this for years.

  Adesola exits, shaking his head.

Remi How is he?

Toye He's fine.

Remi I thought he'd be at work.

Toye Ah, nah, he . . . He had a day off.

Remi Right.
Toye But he's been feelin better recently.

Remi That's good.

Toye Yeah . . .

–

I've gotta practise the piano.

Remi I can stick around and –

Toye Nah, I've gotta concentrate.
  You'll start talkin bout how SUGA plays the –

Remi Alright, alright, I'm gone.

Toye I'll catch you later.

Remi Yeah, course.

  Remi heads out.

Later.

Toye Yeah.

Remi exits.
Toye goes to his piano and plays the Sonata.
But, led by his heart, it drifts into his own tune.
It's quite solemn, minor keys in abundance.
He stops.

Focus, Toye.
Focus.

He plays the Sonata.
Stops suddenly.

I wanna get it pitch perfect,
    but I keep glitchin.
    My mind's spinnin.
    I keep thinkin bout . . .
    About the people we're forgettin.
    Whose voices are disappearin
    cos we look at the MLKs
    the Malcolm Xes
    Rosa Parks of the world.
    I shrugged off the thing
    bout the Michelin star
    but that's a man that's gone far
    and yet I don't know him.
    That's subpar, man.
    There're more shades to us than
    we've been told.
    Doesn't that limit our view of the –

Toye, focus.

He plays again.

How can we grow in our knowledge
    of what it means to be Black?
    Here.
    Black, here.

24

I keep going
   and I wanna be enjoyin it
   cos I love the keys –
   they've always been an escape,
   my friend –
   but the unease won't leave
   even when I say please.

So I buy some books.

He presents the books he's bought.
   They include Why I'm No Longer Talking to White
People About Race, Natives, The Good Immigrant, There
Ain't No Black in the Union Jack, *etc.*
   He picks up the first and begins to read through it.

I wanna learn.
   I'm yearnin for some info.
   My parents didn't gimme the facts
   like Remi's have,
   so I try to dive into it myself.

Flicks through the pages.

It's mad interesting.

Time passes.

Mad arresting.

Adesola enters.

Adesola What're you doing, Toye?

Toye Par[don] –
   I, er, I'm reading.

Adesola It's late.

Toye I know, I –
Adesola You should go to bed.

Toye I will.

Adesola (*re: the book*) What is that?

Toye Huh?

Adesola What are you reading?

Toye shows him the cover.

Is this for school?

Toye nods enthusiastically.

Okay.

Adesola exits.

Toye I keep readin
Readin
Readin.

FOUR

School playground.
Toye, Ash, and Remi hang out.

Toye What do you two wanna do?

Ash What'd you mean?

Toye Like when you're older.

Ash You already –
Remi I wanna have fun.

Remi laughs.

Toye I'm serious.

Remi Finance, innit.
And Ash is gonna sell houses.

Ash Mansions.

Toye Is that really what you wanna do?

Remi Course.

Ash Gotta make that P.

Remi Right?
Toye Forget about money for a minute and –

Ash How can we forget bout money?

Toye I just –
Remi Makes the world go round, bro.

Toye I know, but –

Remi No buts.

Toye I'm bein serious.

Remi Me too.
    You like livin round here?

–

Didn't think so.

Ash Money's the only way we're getting out, Toye.

Remi Only way to get freedom.

Ash That's the goal.

Toye (*to Remi*) Why'd you even wanna work in finance?

Remi Cos it's lit.

Toye I'm serious.

Remi So am I.
    I've read bare books bout it.

Ash She gets gassed over maths.

Remi Stats, solving problems.

Ash It's kinda weird, really.

Remi Shut up, Ash.

Toye You love it?

Remi Yeah.
It's exciting.

Toye (*to Ash*) And d'you love real estate?

Ash Yeah, I . . .
Why?

Toye Cos I've been thinkin
and I don't think I wanna be a doctor no more.

Ash For real?

Toye Yeah.
Remi Why not?

Toye I dunno.
I was thinkin bout your dad's friend, Rem, and I –

Remi What friend?

Toye The chef.

Remi Okay . . .
Toye And I was like, what do I love?
What can I make my stamp in, y'know?

Ash But you like science.

Toye I like everything,
but that ain't the question.
It's bout love.

Ash Right.
Remi Right.
Toye And I love challenging perceptions.

Remi That ain't a job.
Toye It's what I –

Ash laughs, Toye rolls his eyes.

28

Toye I know.
　　My point was: that's what I love about the piano.
　　There's a way of doing things,
　　but you can shake it up.
　　Make it exciting.
　　Change the story, y'know?

Ash So you wanna play piano?

Remi I mean, it makes sense, you're auditionin for –

Toye No. I . . . I wanna be an activist.

Ash and Remi look at one another confused.

Remi And they correlate, how?

Toye I've been reading and reading
　　and piano aside
　　it's the only thing that's got me mad excited.
　　And I wanna make a change.

Ash You would as a doctor.

Remi Literally.

Toye But I wouldn't enjoy it.

Ash You don't know that.

Toye Yeah, I do.
　　I only wanted to do that
　　cos it's all my parents ever spoke about.
　　But it's hard work.
　　And if I've gotta work hard,
　　I'd rather focus on making a change.

Remi Then become a teacher.

Toye A teacher?
　　They're part of the problem.

Remi That ain't true.

Toye In *Natives*, Akala spoke about his teachers –

Remi That's one person.

Toye It ain't though, is it?

Remi Teachers help and support.

Toye I know your dad's one, but you don't need to –

Ash Toye.
Remi It ain't bout that.

Ash Guys.
Toye I mean, I'm pretty sure –

Ash Bein an activist sounds kinda cool.

Toye Right?

Remi It ain't meant to be 'cool'.

Ash You know what I mean.

Remi What'll your goals be?

Toye What?

Remi As an activist.
　　What're you fighting for?

Toye Awareness.
　　Like you gave me.

Remi *I* gave you?
Toye When you spoke about your dad's friend.
　　The Michelin star.

Remi And that made you wanna be an activist?

Toye Yeah and weirdly it opened my eyes.
　　I never thought about Black chefs.
　　I mean, I know we cook – have stalls,
　　shops, catering businesses –
　　but I looked up the Michelin star

and that's next level.
It opened my mind, Rem.

Remi Wow. You're serious.

Toye Yeah.
And I wonder who else is just wandering around
thinking that to be great they gotta be on MLK's wave –

Ash Do you think I only wanna become a real estate agent
cos my brother's doin that?

–

Toye Probably.

Remi Do you love it?

Ash I dunno.

Remi You're always watchin those
micro-house videos on TikTok.

Ash But sellin's a whole different thing.
I never really considered my options.

Toye That's what I'm sayin.
Not many people –

The bell goes.

Remi We should get to class.

Ash I really can't be bothered.

Remi You'll get beats if you bunk, Ash.

Ash I know, obv I'm gonna go.
Just bored of learnin from ancient textbooks.

Remi Ash, c'mon –

Toye She's right.
They ain't teachin
what we need to know, Rem.

Remi Then, like my dad says, speak to the teacher.
That's what I do if I'm unhappy with –

Toye Or we could start our own thing.

Remi What?
Ash Like what?

Toye Like, I dunno, a school.
Teachin everyone what they *should* be learnin
in addition to –

Ash Can we do that?

Toye I dunno.
But we should try.
Then we'd have a voice.

Ash That could be sick.

Remi Ash, don't entertain his –

Ash Rem, he's right.

Toye Thank you.
If we start realisin our potential,
what we could do in life
outside the basic boxes
they build for us.

Ash You gotta plan?

Toye Yeah, but I want you guys to do it with me.
You in?

FIVE

School playground.
Toye, Remi and Ash enthusiastically teach their first lesson.

Toye Hey, everyone, I'm glad you came.
This was random
and I know it's break
so thank you.
I wanted us to come together
to talk about people we might not know.
Black people who've added
so much to the country.
So we can expand our minds,
sprint from the images
stereotypes.

Remi, Ash and I have been readin
learnin bout people
who've done amazing
brilliant things.
And it affects us all.

If we don't know these things,
we just keep walking around
with half-empty glasses.
When you're parched
in a desert –
and trust me, we are –
that ain't enough.

Remi On that note –

Toye (*laughs*) The first person we'll speak about is . . .

Ash Margaret Busby.

Remi How many of you know her?

Toye We just learnt about her
but she's someone we should all know.

Remi In 1967, she became Britain's youngest book publisher.

Toye She set up the company with Clive Allison,
     working outta his friend's flat.

Ash They had no money
     but sought to make their work
     accessible.

Toye Affordable.

Remi Going out on the streets
     stopping people.

Ash But people assumed she was an assistant.
     There to make the tea,
     not a driving force behind the company.

Remi The UK's first Black female publisher.

Toye In 1969, Busby published her first novel –
     The Spook Who Sat by the Door,
     a novel rejected by forty American publishers.

Remi And it became a great success.

Ash It was translated into six languages.

Toye Adapted for film.

Remi And there was fear it would start race warfare.

Toye She persisted through the hard times
     not caring about what would 'sell'
     but stories she felt needed to be told.

Remi Busby said she 'was being treated as some sort of
freak' –
     'the girl from Ghana goes into publishing'

Toye . . . as if they were saying: 'Black girl can read.'

Ash W.H. Allen bought her company in 1987
     but couldn't find a job for her.

Toye But she didn't let that stop her.
　　She continued to get voices out into the world.

Remi And is now best known for
　　her 1992 anthology
　　Daughters of Africa.

Ash Which included writing by women
　　of African descent from ancient Egypt
　　to the present.

Remi Her influence is apparent in the fact that
　　Zadie Smith – arguably this country's
　　most acclaimed Black writer –
　　says Margaret changed the landscape
　　of UK publishing and arts coverage.

Toye Says that we owe Margaret Busby.

SIX

Toye's bedroom.
　　Toye and Ash sit on their phones, while eating snacks.

Ash Everyone's gassed.

Toye Mmm.
Ash It's mad.

Toye Mmm.

Ash Olive said it should be longer.

–

Josh agrees.

–

Fawzia and –
　　You listenin?

Toye Yeah.

Ash What's wrong?
   Did you feel like we weren't strong enough?

Toye What?

Ash I mean, our performance.

Toye Did you think that?

Ash Nah, I . . .

Toye Ash.

Ash It was a bit chaotic.

Toye We were having fun.
Ash And I also – I know.

–

Ash We could also think about –

Toye About what?

Ash I was about to say.

–

Think bout telling a story.

Toye This ain't English.

Ash It's what all the best activists do, Toye.

–

Like, why did you choose Margaret Busby?

Toye Cos she was interesting.

Ash Is that enough?

Toye Yeah.
Ash Cos I think there should be something
   more personal, y'know.

Toye She's Black.
I'm Black.
That's personal.

Ash Well, it just seemed like fun facts you can google.
Why would anyone spend their lunch break listening to
that?

Toye But they did.

Ash Cos it was the first one.
They were intrigued.
They'll get bored of it quickly though.

Toye Why you bein so bad mind?

Ash I ain't.
Just wantin to shake it up.

Toye We just started.

Ash Yeah, so we should try different strategies.

Toye Like . . .

Ash I dunno.
Obviously, we should try and connect to the person.
What makes us want to teach about them.

Toye Cool.

Ash (*picking up her notebook*) But I was also thinking, like,
we could look at a different continent each time.

Toye What?

Ash To highlight different moments in history.

Toye I wanna focus on Black people.

Ash Yeah, I . . .
I know.
There are Black people everywhere.

Toye I know, but –

Ash Do you know bout Madam C.J. Walker?

Toye I dunno, I –

Ash First Black female millionaire.

Toye The one on Netflix?

Ash Yeah.

Toye She's American.

Ash I know.
Toye I don't wanna do Americans.

Ash Why not?

Toye This is bout being *here*.

Ash It all connects.
Toye We can add Americans in later,
  if we have to,
  but we've gotta limit it
  or it'll become so cliché.
  I'm tryna avoid the obvious names.

Ash Do you know about Charles Drew?

Toye Nah, I –

Ash His research into the storage,
  processing, and shipment of blood plasma
  saved the lives of hundreds of Britons during World War
Two.

Toye That's what I want.

Ash He's American.

Toye I –

  There's a buzz.

(*Exiting.*) I'll get it!

  He goes.

Ash Ugggh.
It's fine, Ash.
Just Toye bein Toye.
He'll come around to –

Toye returns.

Toye I don't want Americans.

Ash But it's –

Toye I know it'll be harder,
but we've gotta focus on people here.

Ash Fine.

Toye That ain't what I was thinkin bout anyway.

Ash What was it?

Toye You mentioned Josh, Olive, Fawzia.

Ash Yeah.
Toye What do they all have in common?

Ash Olive, Josh, and Fawzia?

Toye Yeah.

Ash I . . .
I dunno.

–

They all do History?

Toye Olive doesn't.

Ash She does Sociology.

Toye Okay, but what d'they have in common?

Ash Just tell me.

Toye They're all Black.

Ash I thought that's what you wanted.

Toye No, I . . .
I mean, it's fine.
It's good,
but other people need to learn too.

Ash I thought it was about making people see
the possibilities.

Toye Yeah, but in my readin it said
it's good for other people
to get insight too,
so they stop thinkin so narrowly.

Ash We could take it a step at a time.

Toye No, we need to get to everyone now.
Our school's mad mixed –
Black
White
Asian –

A knock.

Toye It shouldn't – It's open!
Ash Middle Eastern.

Toye What'd you say?

Ash Nothing.

Toye Yeah, you –

Remi enters.

Remi Wagwan.
Toye My point is, this is useful for everyone.
Ash Hey, Rem, where've you been?

Toye Yeah, why'd you tell us to come without you?

Remi Mr Barry called me into his office.

Toye Why?
Ash For what?

Remi To ask what we were doing at lunch.

Toye It's none of his business.

Remi It's his school.

Toye And why couldn't he just ask me?

Remi Cos I'm Head Girl.

Toye Right.
Remi Was saying:
  'A Head Girl shouldn't be gathering crowds.'

Ash He's so jarring, man.

Toye Right?
Remi Yeah, but he had a point, y'know?

Toye How?

Remi We shouldn't really be doin it during school.

Toye When else are we gonna get everyone together?

Remi I'm just saying, crowds have the potential for danger.

Toye You're acting like we're in the O2.

Remi We could just do it after school.

Ash After school.
Toye I'm too busy, Rem.

Remi It's your passion project though.

Toye Tell Mr Barry that –

Remi I ain't his messenger.

Toye *As Head Girl*, tell him it's important.

Remi He knows that.

Ash Does he?
Toye He does?

Remi Yeah, I told him why we were doin it.

Toye But he doesn't care.

Remi It ain't that.

Toye Whatever it is, convince him it's for –

Remi Guys, I've tried, I . . .
    We could ask for an assembly.

Ash D'you think he'd –
Toye Nah. Then it becomes the school's
    and they ain't been doing this work so far
    so I ain't givin them the credit.

Remi We should listen to him.

Toye If you're so worried about being Head Girl
    you don't have to continue, y'know?

Remi Ain't bout that.

Toye No?

Remi No.

Toye Ash says people are buzzin bout this, Rem.

Ash They are.
Toye We can't give up just cos Mr Barry says.

Remi He's always been reasonable.

Toye In what world?
Ash Not always.

Remi Toye, c'mon.
    He created the International Day we have.

Toye One day every June.

Ash It's kinda sick though.

Toye I know, I love it, but –
Ash All the food and the –

Remi And it's more than we got before he started.
    Who says he won't give us more?

Toye Rem, I get it.
    You're Head Girl.
    You don't wanna mess that up.
    And we ain't gonna.

–

You don't have to do this.
    I won't get mad.

Remi I just think we could either collaborate with –

Toye Rem, you can step back if –

Remi This is meant to be fun, Toye.

Toye Exactly.
    How's bringin Mr Barry in gonna be fun?

–

–

Ash You guys wanna go hoop?

Remi Yes, please.
Toye I can't.

Remi Toye, c'mon.

Ash Don't be upset by –

Toye I ain't, I just . . . I don't wanna leave my dad alone.

Remi Ain't he alone all day?

Toye Exactly.

–

Remi Fine, we can chill here and –

Toye Nah, you guys go.

Ash You sure?

Toye Yeah.

–

Ash Cool.

Remi We'll see you tomorrow.

Toye Yeah.

Remi Later.
Ash See you.

Toye Safe.

Ash and Remi leave.

That was a lie,
   but I need some piano time.
   Can't forget about the audition.
   Not when this school can open doors,
   gimme new opportunities.

He presses a key on the piano.

I love this feeling, y'know?

He riffs on the piano, playing a playful melody.
   Laughs to himself.

The flow's sick, ain't it?
   But I've gotta focus on . . .

The Sonata. He plays that.

I play and play and play.
   The last hour on replay.
   The conversations of today.
   And I realise,
   Mr Barry's tryna persuade us to stop.
   So he can stay on top.
   Pretending he can give us what we need,
   but what they feed us at school ain't a good balance.

What started this all was MLK.
　　The fact that that's all we hear
　　and I couldn't bear to any longer.
　　But Remi's right in some way,
　　except what we need from the school's
　　gotta be stronger than an assembly.
　　That's too small for our need.

That's what's keeping our glasses half-empty.

So I read.
　　Looking for a tool.
　　Read.
　　Digging for water.
　　Read.
　　It's gruelling but I must . . .

His eyes close, but he forces them open.

Read.

His head flops down, but he forces it up.

Read.

Adesola enters.

Adesola Toye.

Toye Read.

Adesola (*seeing the books*) For school?

Toye (*just realising Adesola's there*) Yeah.

Adesola I'm sure it's not so important that you can't –

Toye Yeah, it –

His head flops down, but he forces it up.

Adesola Go to sleep, Toye.

Adesola flicks the light off and exits.
　　Toye turns his phone flash on and continues reading.

Toye Read.
Read.
Read.
Filling my glass.
Filling my glass.
Filling my glass.

SEVEN

A montage. Toye, Ash and Remi research, teach, and go through life.

Remi Diane Abbott.

Ash Walter Tull.

Remi First Black woman elected to Parliament.

Ash First Black army officer to lead white troops into battle.

Toye That a good thing?

Remi He was a hero.

Toye But war?

Ash He was also a football player.
Remi It's not like we're promoting war.

Toye He was?

Ash Yeah.
Remi Yeah, he's bare –

–

Remi Let's hoop.

Toye No, let's find more names.

Ash You keep rejecting them.

Toye That ain't true.

46

Remi We need a break.

Ash Innit.

Toye Later.

–

Remi Fanny Eaton.

Ash Naomi Campbell.

Remi No.

Ash Why not?

Remi She ain't historical.

Toye Neither's Diane Abbott.

Remi But she's a model.

Toye I guess.

Ash Nah, that ain't fair, she's –

Remi What bout Mary Seacole?

Ash We learnt a bit bout her already, so do we wanna –

–

Toye Thanks for coming back.
    Today we're gonna look at the life of –

–

I need to go to music.

Ash You're still doin that?

Toye My parents are paying for classes, I can't just –

Remi You know you'll miss this if you go to that school?

Ash He ain't goin nowhere.
    He can't now.

–

Toye Claudia Jones.

Remi Olaudah Equiano.

Ash Trevor McDonald.

–

Remi I can't do this any more.

Toye Why not?
Ash Rem, you –

Remi I've got too much revision.
Toye Is this bout Mr Barry?

Remi No, I just –

Ash Don't let him get into your head.

Remi I'm sorry.
  I just –

–

Toye Fanny Eaton.

Ash Linford Christie.

Toye Dr Harold Moody.

–

Ash I still think we should do Naomi Campbell.

Toye Ash.

Ash Do you know what she did for the fashion industry?
  That world changes ours bares.

Toye I know, but –

–

Toye Naomi Campbell.
Ash Naomi Campbell.

–

Remi You guys wanna hoop?

Toye We can't.

Ash I can.

Toye Ash, we need to continue.

Ash Don't you have piano soon?

Toye Ain't going.

Ash For real?

Toye Yeah.

Remi Ash? You hoopin?

Ash Sorry, Rem.

Remi Seriously? I –

–

Toye Who should we do next?

EIGHT

School playground.
  Toye and Ash teach.

Toye Have you guys ever helped someone out
  and watch them get all the praise
  when they do it well?

–

It can be jarring, can't it?

Ash That's kinda how we imagine
  the person we're talking about today might feel.

Toye He was a teacher.

Ash And, sure, part of being a teacher is your students
  flying. Ideally.

Toye But when you significantly help Charles Darwin.

Ash You'd think more people would know your part in the story.

Toye But how many of us know . . .

Toye looks off, distracted.

Ash John Edmonstone.

Toye Yeah, he . . . He was . . .

Ash Darwin's teacher at Edinburgh University.
Where his expertise become invaluable for –

Toye But this ain't bout Darwin.

Ash No. You could go to class for that.

Toye This is bout Edmon—

Remi enters.

Remi Sorry everyone, but we're not allowed crowds in the playground.
Could we break this up?

Toye Really, Rem?

–

Remi Sorry.

–

Toye I never get why people choose to be opps?
I'm here tryna help make change
and Remi's actin like I'm a deranged cult leader.
Ain't my fault people value my words,
actually like discussin all this,
find some bliss in not being lied to.
Yet she just shuts it down.
Embarrassin me in front of everyone,
when she could've pulled me aside.

Oppressin us, when she could've just
stayed along for the ride.
It's a madness, really.
Obliteratin all the work we put in.
We didn't even just post a message online
to get people here.
We went up to each person.
Harder work, but we had to grin and bear it,
cos we knew that'd be more personal.
They'd feel like we heard em.
For it all to go in a second?
It's absurd.
Is this how ants feel when we stomp on em?

–

It ain't fair.
And I ain't gonna take it.
This is a movement.

NINE

Toye's sitting room.
Toye paces up and down, as Ash flicks through her notebook.

Toye We need to escalate it.

Ash Whaddya –
Toye We need bigger change.

Ash Bigger change?

Toye Especially if Mr Barry's tryna get in our way.

Ash Whaddya –

Toye Protests.

Ash What?

Toye We need to protest.

Ash For?

Toye Equality.
    Us to be seen the same.

Ash That weren't the plan.

Toye It should be.
    I've been readin more.
    Baldwin.
    Davis.
    Coates.
    Kendi.
    Lettin the Americans in.
    Learnin more bout the big picture.
    The methods.
    And this ain't enough.
    Changin our mentality is tough
    if we don't change society simultaneously.
    Change the curriculum.

Ash We'll get in trouble if we –

Toye That's fine.

Ash Toye, we can't –

Toye Wales are doin it.

Ash Doin what?
Toye Incorporating Black history into each subject.

Ash Then we could do the assembly, like Remi said.

Toye You really think that's enough?

–

Exactly.
    We could do what they did at Pimlico.

Ash What?

Toye I just read about it.
  There was discrimination.
  They were sayin hijabs shouldn't be
  'too colourful',
  even though other clothing
  could be any colour.
  Hair couldn't
  'block the views of others',
  aka afros.
  And that's just uniform policy.
  They also –

Ash What did the students do, Toye?

Toye I was getting there.

–

They resisted till their headteacher resigned.

Ash You want Mr Barry to resign?

Toye He ain't goin with the times.
Ash He ain't that bad.

Toye He's silent.

Ash They'll never get rid of him.

Toye Imagine having a Black headteacher.

Ash Mr Barry turned our school around.
  Grades have shot up since he started.
  Less exclusions.

Toye That's all superficial if we don't get societal change.

Ash Where'd you read that?

Toye School's meant to prep us for the future.
  Not just get us to pass exams.

Ash I know, but –

Toye You don't have to be involved.
　　Go speak to Mr Barry, like Remi does.

Ash It ain't one or the other, Toye.

Toye Except it is.

–

Ash If we're goin that far, we've gotta expand.

Toye I . . .

Ash I wanna bring my culture in too.

Toye That ain't –
Ash And others' too.
　　It can't just be about Black British culture.

Toye But that's what –
Ash You know Yasha Asley,
　　an Iranian boy,
　　got an A in GCSE maths
　　at eight years old.

Toye Why was he doing that at eight years old?

Ash That ain't the point.
Toye He should've been having –

Ash Toye.

Toye I don't wanna learn about eight-year-olds doing –

Ash That ain't what I'm saying.
　　You know that.

Toye I wanna do this my way, Ash.
　　This is about Black history.

Ash So everyone else gets pushed to the side?
　　You never even asked what I wanted to bring to this.

Toye What do you wanna bring to this, Ash?

Ash An understanding that my history's been erased,
  altered, too.

Toye Gosh.

Ash Toye.

Toye You guys weren't even colonised.

Ash That didn't protect us.
  We had our own strikes and protests
  when the UK –
  the *great* Winston Churchill –
  came for our oil.
  Orchestrated a coup
  to get our Prime Minister
  outta their way.
  Stifling us, and –

Toye And that's important.

Ash Thanks for letting me know, Toye.

Toye Don't get like that.

Ash Like what?

Toye All I'm sayin is I don't wanna
  'all lives matter' what I'm doing.

Ash It's called inclusion.

Toye That's how they dilute our stories.

Ash And it's okay to dilute mine?

Toye I ain't stoppin you from doing –

Ash From what?
  Going my own way?
  I'm one of the few Middle Eastern people at our school.
  If we segregate ourselves in that way
  how're we making progress?

Toye You've got a privilege I don't, Ash.
  Your skin is –

Ash And you've got a privilege I don't, Toye.
  You were born here.
  Have bare family here.
  My family had to upend our lives
  eight years ago.
  So call it 'all lives matter' if you want
  but I'm just tryna not fade into the background
  like I've always done.
  Like I always do.
  At home.
  School.
  Everywhere.
  If I'm gonna protest,
  risk gettin in trouble –

Toye Do you wanna be an ally or not?

Ash Don't, Toye.

Toye You don't have to help if you don't wanna.

Ash It's fine.
  I get it.
  I just thought cos we're friends,
  you'd be open to my ideas –

Toye I am.

Ash Nah.
  You may be friends with me and Rem
  but you're just like the other leaders.
  Pushin women to the side
  when we carry these things.

Toye C'mon, Ash. It ain't like that.

Ash Nah?
  Who did the most research?
  Who gave you feedback –

Toye I'm sorry, Ash.
You're important to this.
We're like Keem and Kendrick, man.

Ash And I guess you're Kendrick?
The one that'll fly
then reach back and support?
Nah, don't flatter yourself
you wouldn't put anyone on but you.

Ash leaves.

Toye I'm glad she walked out.
Really.
Cos I actually don't have time for this.
I've gotta practise.

He plays the Sonata.
Ash and Remi enter, in a different space to Toye.

Ash He's being dumb.

Remi You surprised?
Ash I wasn't even tryna take away from him.
I just, there are five Middle Eastern people in our school.
Five. Out of sixteen hundred.
How can I do my own thing?
It won't be nearly as effective.
And, yeah, maybe I shouldn't have –

Remi Ash, it's calm.

Ash It ain't though.
This school was important.

Remi You think I don't know that?
I liked doin it too.

Ash Then why'd you stop it?

Remi It wasn't me.

Ash Has my memory gone hazy?

Remi You know what I mean.
Ash It's your fault he's going mad.
  Now talking bout
  protesting.

Remi Protesting?
Ash Doing what they did in Pimlico.

Remi What'd they do in –
Ash Which wasn't even the plan.
  The school was the plan.
  Educating people.
  Expanding their minds, not –

Remi Ash, chill.

Ash I am.

Remi Toye's just actin out cos he's going through it.

Ash Ain't we all?
Remi I think his dad's gettin sicker.

Ash For real?

Remi Couldn't you tell?

Ash No, I –

Remi Just don't take it personally.
  You did a great job.

Ash You think?

Remi Yeah. You killed it every single time.

  Ash smiles at Remi, getting emotional.
    They hug.
    Toye stops playing.

Toye No, I can't.
  I have to prepare.
  Read more,
  if I'm gonna do this on my own.

TEN

School gates.
  Toye hands out flyers.

Toye Don't go to your classes
    where your glasses are left half-empty.
    Come to our History talk,
    get our vision twenty-twenty,
    so we don't get trapped
    in this institutional penitentiary.

  Ash enters.

Ash That's a bit long, ain't it?

Toye I –
Ash It should probably be catchier.

Toye Don't go to your classes
    where your glasses are left half-empty.
    Come to our History talk,
    get our vision twenty-twenty.

–

How's that?

Ash (*shrugs*) Alright.

–

I didn't wanna leave things on a bad note.

Toye Well, you stormed outta my house.

–

Ash I thought you weren't doin the talks.

Toye I ain't.
    But I have to get everyone together
    so they know what the plan is.

  Remi enters, holding one of Toye's flyers.

Remi Toye, I don't –

Toye Jeez, what now?

Remi I just ain't sure you should be doin this.

Toye Rem, if you don't wanna –

Remi Mr Barry pulled me aside again, y'know?
    To ask me what you're doing.

Ash What'd you tell him?

Remi Nothin but whatever you're planning –

Toye (*to Ash*) Did you tell her bout the protest?

Ash No, I just –

Toye For real?

Ash She's my friend.

Toye And then you come tryna speak to me.

Ash Cos I want us to –

Toye (*to Remi*) I'm doin this for us, Rem.

Remi No one asked you to be our voice.

Toye I'm just tryna educate us.
Ash Guys, let's not get into it.

Remi Ash, stay outta this.
Toye Ash, it's fine. I can handle Remi.

Ash I'm a part of it, I –
Remi Handle me? I know your dad's sick but –

    Ash walks away from them.

Ash Really? Cool, I'm gonna –
Toye I'm tryna get people to pay attention.

Remi To what?

Toye To how dumb this all is.

Remi It ain't dumb.

Toye We're all stuck
and you know why that –

Remi Who's stuck, Toye?
I ain't.
Bares of us ain't.

Toye Is that why people were gassed bout my class?

Remi They also like going to their actual classes, so –

Toye Cos they're conditioned to.
But they don't teach us bout the real world.

Remi What'd you know bout the real world?
You think our teachers ain't lived out there?

Toye I wouldn't have taken you for an opp, y'know?

Remi An opp?

Toye Must be.
Remi I didn't even tell him bout a protest,
or whatever it is you wanna do.
He just asked what was goin on, so I . . .
I just told him what you're goin through.
Bout your dad.

Toye This has nothin to do with him.

Remi No?

Toye No. I care bout this movement.

Remi I ain't sayin you don't, but –
Toye Bout what we're going through.
It's got nothin to do with my dad.
Ain't every day that something bad
leads us to fight, y'know?
Especially when you've been seein
stuff online

all the time
and keep pushin it to the side
for piano, friends, ease.

Remi You're hurtin.

Toye I can't believe Mr Barry's got you
wrapped
round his finger.
You ain't even thinkin
your own thoughts,
just stayin silent so they
see you as a saint.

Remi Just cos I ain't in the playground
making loud sounds of protest
don't mean I'm silent, Toye.
There's just a way you play this game.
Get to the top then change things.

Toye Your dad tell you that?

Remi My dad fights mad hard, man.
Ain't as simple as you like to think.

Toye If you fold now, Rem,
you won't suddenly be bold
when you reach the top.

Remi You know what –

Remi walks away from Toye.

Toye Rem, don't walk away from me.

Remi You ain't listenin.

Toye Walk away from me an' we're done, man.

Remi stops.

Remi Ain't we already done?

Toye I want you on our team.

Remi I thought I was an opp.

Toye I just . . .
Remi But I don't need to be 'radical', Toye.
   It's sad.

Toye They teach the same thing.
   Year after year,
   like they're scared of change.
   Parliament said it's for schools
   and teachers
   to decide what topics
   resources
   they use to reach out to us.

Remi And you believe them?

Toye No, but –

Remi Exactly.
Toye We could try it.
   We built so much in this world, you know?
   We were pioneers in
   philosophy
   science
   literature
   so much more.
   But how many of those people can I name?
   We never learn that
   but it shapes our identities.
   The way we think.
   What we love.
   How we're loved.
   What we need ain't being given to us.
   Not even to the white kids,
   cos they'll grow up livin a lie.

Remi You wanna change the curriculum?
   Okay, let's say, we get to English.
   No Black authors in ours.

A couple in my dad's.
I asked him bout that.
He said for every article written about Malorie Blackman
there are a million about Harper Lee.
We won't get the breadth of research we need.
And teachers don't get affected by that.
Yeah, sure, they might get students with lower grades
and lose their jobs,
but they can do other things.
They've got their degrees.
But if they switch it up, *we're* affected.
This is bigger than school, Toye.
Bigger than teachers,
so while you're so busy being a preacher
you don't even see that they wish they could help
but are equally trapped.
You talk bout half-empty glasses
but it's about how you see it.
As an opportunity or a hindrance.
But you keep choosin to see it as half-empty.
You keep choosin to –

Toye I ain't gettin into a debate bout this, Rem.
If you wanna tell Mr Barry something,
something real
tell him I'm gonna protest.

Remi You better be careful who you cross, Toye.

Toye You're an opp, so –

Remi Stop callin me that.

Toye It's what you are.

Remi pushes Toye.
    Toye pushes Remi back.
    Remi grabs him by the collar.
    Toye does the same, when Ash runs in and pulls them apart.

Ash Hey, guys, chill.
  CHILL.

–

What're you doin?

Remi He started it.

Toye You pushed me an' you're tryna –

Remi Told you not to call me an opp.

Ash Guys, stop.
  You're friends.

Toye No, you were right, Rem,
  we're done.

Ash Toye, you –

Remi Ash, it's fine.
  I'm gone.

  Remi heads off.

Ash Rem, you don't –

Toye Leave her.

Ash What's wrong with you?

Toye Me?

  Ash heads off.

You really goin after her?

Ash She's my friend.

Toye And I ain't?

Ash Toye, don't –

Toye You know what? Never mind.
  I've gotta go to my music lesson anyway.

Ash You're still doin that?

Toye Why wouldn't I?

Ash laughs and shakes her head.

Ash You're doin all this
and then you're gonna audition
for a scholarship to a private school?

Toye They've gotta sick music –

Ash A sick music department.
You said.
But then you go and tell us to fight.
Shake it all up.
Disrupt.
Dismantle.
Then you're gonna dip?

Toye I'll still –
Ash You're a hypocrite.
If you were so for this 'fight'
you'd give up the idea of that school.

Toye I'll still help.

Ash You barely had time for our friendship.
You paid me and Rem dust, suddenly only
speaking to us when you needed something
and you think you're gonna go
and keep fighting?

Toye I –

Ash Nah.
You don't need to answer to me.

Ash exits.
  Toye stands there, shocked.
  *He stares at his piano, then touches it, contemplating
her words.*

ELEVEN

Toye's sitting room.
  Toye plays the Sonata.
  Midway through, he stops.
  Plays an angry tune.
  Adesola enters and Toye goes back to the Sonata.

Adesola Your headteacher called.

Toye (*moving closer*) Par[don] –

Adesola Your headteacher called.
  He said you've been causing trouble.

Toye That ain't –

Adesola Is he lying then?

–

He said you're breaking rules
  and that you're on a third strike.

Toye What? I ain't done –

Adesola Haven't.
  Speak properly.

–

Toye Why's everyone on me?
  I haven't done anything.
  This isn't fair.

Adesola Do you know what isn't fair?
  Having to answer the phone
  cos your mum's at work
  and struggling to pick it up as it
  rings and rings and rings.

And when you finally get it,
  you have to hear people

say they're sorry to hear about your condition.
Then their continual use of the word
'pardon',
cos I think they've heard
but my voice is being destroyed.
I'm not myself.
I don't own my body any more.

And then being told your son
is acting out
and they don't want him around
if he continues that way.

It's hard to beg
when you know it's pointless.
When there's not enough energy
or volume for it to be felt.
It's embarrassing
and that's not fair, Toye.

You need to grow up.

Toye I'm just tryna make a change.

Adesola A change?

Toye Our school doesn't teach us about Black history.

Adesola So you want to be excluded because of that?

Toye I'm trying to use my voice.

Adesola Don't.

Toye I have to.
    I . . .

Toye breaks into tears, surprising Adesola.

Adesola Toye.

Toye (*wiping them away*) I'm fine.

Adesola What's wrong?

Toye Nothing.

Adesola Nothing?

Toye I just . . . There's so much to do, Dad.
  I just wanna fill up our glasses.
  Change the curriculum,
  the leadership,
  get more Black teachers.

Adesola And you want to do *all* that?

Toye It's important.

Adesola You're sixteen.
  You need to focus on your studies.

Toye But no one else is focusing on it, so who's gonna –

Adesola I hope you've still being practising the piano.

Toye Yeah, but I . . . I don't wanna do the audition any more.

Adesola Toye.

Toye I need to stay at school.

Adesola You've been asking for this for a long time.

Toye I know, but . . .
  It's gonna be worse there.

Adesola We've paid for the audition.

Toye I know, I . . .

Adesola You'll be fine.
  You'll do well.
  You always do.

Adesola exits.
  Toye takes a deep breath.
  He looks at his books. Puts them away.

**Toye No one understands, so I don't bother any more.
  Even I can't escape the structures.**

This teaching is known.
This story is known.
This failure common.
My glory thrown in a ditch.

I don't speak to Ash or Remi.
I play the same old melody on my piano.
It doesn't even bring me the same joy it once did.
I don't feel half-empty any more.
Just empty.

But teachers, Mr Barry, are happy with this.
Me handing in my homework on time,
taking information in without challenging their minds.
My piano tutor says I'm playing better than ever.
Maybe this is how it's meant to be:
playing to their chords.
Livin within conventions.
Livin within restrictions.
Livin within a structure.
Lettin someone write my narrative.

But I don't wanna do that.
I don't wanna . . .
I don't . . .

TWELVE

Private school hall.
  Toye stands with Adesola.

Adesola Are you ready, Toye?

Toye I . . . I dunno.

Adesola You'll be fine.
  You'll do well.

Toye I always do.

Toye sits at the piano.
  Toye stares it.
  Takes a deep breath.
  Then starts the Sonata.
  In between, he stops.

–

He begins to play his own tune.
  He uses chords randomly.
  It doesn't have a rhythm.
  At least not one we're familiar with.
  There's no logic to it.
  He's just freestyling.
  Like all his smaller moments building into one.
  It might be different every single night.
  The most important thing is it shouldn't feel neat or beautiful.
  It's an expression of his mind.

–

–

–

–

–

Toye stands with Adesola.

Adesola Are you ready, Toye?

Toye I . . . I dunno.

Adesola You'll be fine.
  You'll do well.

Adesola exits.

Toye I always do.

Toye lifts his head up.
   Looks around.
   He plays the Sonata.

THIRTEEN

School playground.
   Remi and Ash sit down.

Remi Whaddya wanna start with?

Ash I dunno.

Remi Well you should probably introduce yourself.

Ash Yeah, duh.

–

Ash I'm mad nervous.

Remi You'll be great.

Ash What if no one cares?

Remi They will.
Ash What if –

Remi And what comes after the intro?

Ash I'll talk a bit about my mission statement.

Remi See, it's simple.
Ash How the idea came about –

   Toye enters.

Toye Hey, guys.

–

Ash Hi.
Remi Hey.

Toye I heard you're doing an assembly.

Remi She's allowed to do an assembly.

Toye I didn't say nothing.

Ash It's the first time you've spoken to us in weeks.

Toye Sorry, I've been . . .

Remi You alright?

Toye Yeah.
No, I . . .

Ash Is it your dad?

Toye No, no, I . . .
I'm leavin.

–

Remi You got in?

Toye nods.
Remi and Ash scream in celebration, surprising Toye.

Remi Bro!
Ash Toye!

Remi Ain't you gassed?

Toye Gassed?
I'm abandonin everyone.
I should be doin more.

Remi Ugh.
Why'd you keep tryna carry it all?

Toye Cos no one else is.

Remi You're a baby boy.
Come shoot hoops again.
Listen to BTS.

Toye I never listened to them.

Remi That's why you're always stressed.

Toye Our glasses are still half-empty.

Ash Ain't your job to fill em up.
You provided the table for them to stand on.

Toye That ain't a thing.
Ash Made a change here already.

Toye What change?
Remi She's right.
People couldn't stop talking bout wanting more.

Toye But I'm leavin
Goin to a school that's gonna be even worse
and betrayin the whole –

Remi You still like playin the piano?

Toye Yeah, but I –

Remi Then take it as a win, Toye. Enjoy it.

Toye There's still so much that could be done.

Ash Yeah, I've been researchin
and we're gonna continue.
Just not puttin all the weight on our shoulders.

Toye (*to Remi*) You doin it with her?

Remi Not the assembly, but I'm gonna do something.
I'm just not sure exactly how I wanna fight.
Not yet.

Toye Right.

Remi But there's this group Ash found.

Ash NUS Black Students.
They connect people all over the country
to help do what you've been tryna do.

Toye I didn't know bout that.

Ash Yeah, it's good.

Remi Maybe you can look into that.
  For the new school.

Toye Yeah.

–

–

If I did, maybe we could connect
  and, like,
  share methods?

–

Ash Of course.

Remi But we might disagree.

Ash You two disagree?
  Nah, can't imagine that.

  They laugh.

Toye You really think we'll be able to make a big change?

Ash Someday.

Remi Soon, hopefully.
  But who knows?
  I can feel it, but . . .

Ash You can never know.

Remi No. But we can still sing our song.

FOURTEEN

Toye's sitting room.
  Adesola is sat down, when Toye enters.

Toye Hi, Dad.

  Adesola lifts his hand up to wave.
    Toye gives him a small smile.
    Toye sighs.
    Sits at his piano.
    He turns to Adesola.

Can I show you something?

Adesola (*barely heard*) Okay.

  Toye helps Adesola over to the stool.

Toye How was the nurse?

Adesola She . . .

Toye Tell me using this.
  If you'd like.

  Adesola looks to Toye.
    Taps a key.

Adesola How was school?

  Toye plays the piano.
    A soft, short tune.
    They smile at each other, liking this.

Good.

  The End.